10 TO CUT A POTATO

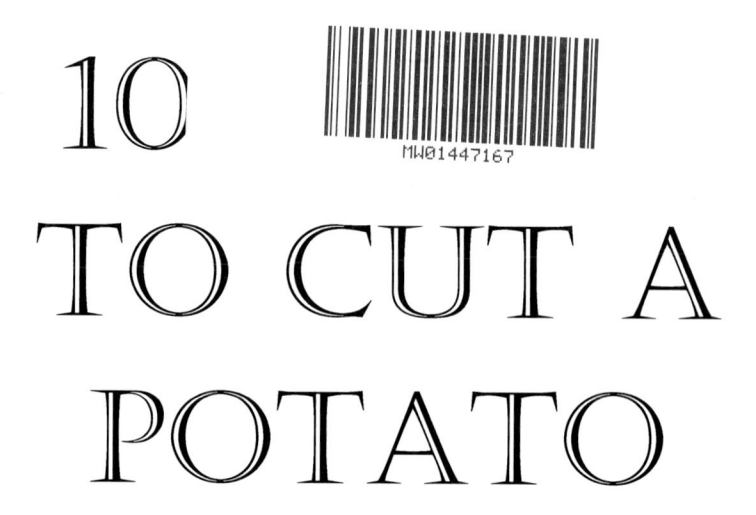

A CREATIVE COOKING GUIDE FOR EXERCISING KNIFE SKILLS

Benjamin James Freeman-Prichard

Copyright 2015 Benjamin James Freeman-Prichard

All Rights Reserved

INTRODUCTION

I love potatoes. In fact, I've actually never met a person who didn't like potatoes. The simple spud is a people pleaser. It holds infinite potential in spatial exploration. It can just as well be simple and nutritious or serve as an excellent delivery device for other foods and flavors.

I discovered very early on that cutting potatoes was a great place to begin my cooking career. My first cooking job I worked in a restaurant within the world's biggest microbrewery. I was hired to cut cases of potato by hand to be used for steak fries, potato wedges and potato skins. Eventually I got fast enough to cut 8 cases in an 8 hour day. My first day working, the Chef asked me to cut a few potatoes in half but he didn't tell me how it was going to be used so I stood it on its edge and cut it in half. He later told me, I cut them the wrong way. I responded knowingly, "There are at least 101 ways to cut a potato, please be clear with me if you're being so specific." From the look on his face, I could tell he doubted my creativity. So soon after to prove a point I purchased my own ten pound bag of Idaho potatoes from a neighborhood super market. I started enthusiastically cutting them just to see what I could do.

Hours later I was surrounded by many mounds of cut potatoes. And because I tried to cut and take pictures as I went along, white potato starch had also spread all around my kitchen as well. Eventually I cleaned everything up and I put all of the potato pieces into a pot of boiling water to cook them until they were tender. I poked the bigger pieces with a fork to test their readiness. The fork passed easily through them so I poured off the potato water which I later turned into a sour dough bread starter. I mashed the potato with a spoon until the paste was consistently smooth. I am proud to say not a single piece of potato was wasted during the experiment.

The goal of this book project is to put together a cohesive piece of work that can be used to inspire future generations of cooks. *101 Ways to Cut a Potato* goes beyond just cutting potatoes, in the index section you will find a list of food that can be prepared using the same numbered cuts listed throughout the book in red ink. For me, the book was a meditation in creative cooking while developing my knife skills. I hope the project inspires you as well.

The potato story is a long one. Listed here are a few important parts pertaining to this book. Potatoes are part of the *Solanaccae Family* of plants often referred to as the Nightshade Family, which also includes such foods as eggplant, tomatoes and peppers among many other vegetables. Potatoes have been cultivated for over 7,000 years beginning in the Andes region of South America. There are an estimated 4,000 different varieties of potato worldwide. Potatoes are currently ranked fourth most abundant stable food eaten worldwide right behind wheat, rice and corn.

Potatoes can be broken into three main classifications. The High, Medium or Low Starch Potatoes. The three main classifications of potatoes include High Starch Potato also known as Mealy Potatoes. The Russet Potato would fall into this high starch category. Low Starch Potato referred to as Waxy Potato which would include Red Potatoes. And lastly Medium Starch Potato are referred to as dual purpose because they are starchy but still retrain their shape when cooked. White Potatoes would be a good example of a dual purpose potato.

You can find a use for potato in most recipes so it is an important food to always have in your kitchen. Potatoes can be stored in a cool, dark place with good ventilation for up to weeks or months at a time. However it is always better to eat them sooner than later. Raw potatoes can be shaped into anything, while the waxy low starch potatoes can withstand some cooking, mealy high starch potatoes become brittle there for they must be handled gently when cooked. The next time you're making a dish think of how the potato should be shaped to better serve the dish you're cooking.

One last thing before diving head first into a world of potato cooking please remember to never eat green potatoes, potato seeds, potato leaves or potato starts because they are all poisonous to some degree. Always soak potatoes in fresh running water to loosen any dirt attached to the skin. Wash the potatoes with a sponge to remove the dirt from the sides and then scrub the skins crevices with a dish brush to remove any leftover dirt sediment before preparing it. Always work safely when operating sharp knives and follow all safety precautions using all the other tools used in this book.

Cutting Tools Photo L to R:
(Cookie Cutter, Paring Knife, Fork, Spoon, Chef Knife, Peeler, Masher, Whisk, Peeler, Mandolin)

101 WAYS TO CUT A POTATO

1. Twice Baked Potato

Soak, wash and scrub a mealy potato clean. Dry it with a towel then rub it with either Canola Oil or any other vegetable oil that withstands high temperatures. 1. Poke the potato multiple times with the tines of a fork to allow the heat to penetrate the flesh so the moisture can escape while it cooks. Wrap the potato completely in tin foil. Bake it in the oven for 60 minutes at 400 degrees Fahrenheit. Increase the time by 15 minutes if you are cooking several potatoes together. Carefully remove the potatoes from the oven. Let the potato cool before cutting it or use a dry hand towel to hold it. 2. Stand the potato up on its side and using a Chef knife cut it all the way in half, lengthwise. 3. Scoop out the insides from the two sides with a spoon.

Photo: Mashed potato

4. Mash the contents of the potato in a bowl, add avocado oil, parmesan cheese, garlic, paprika, salt and pepper. Put the mixture into a piping pastry bag and pipe the mixture back into the potato skins or just spoon it back in. Bake for 15 minutes at 350 degrees Fahrenheit until the potato tops turn golden brown. Garnish with diced chives and red chili pepper flakes.

2. Potato Waves

Soak, wash and scrub a mealy potato clean. Dry the potato and then rub it with vegetable oil. Bake the potato in the oven uncovered for 60 minutes at 400 degree Fahrenheit. 5. Lay the potato down flat then using a chef knife, start from one end and carefully cut an arching up and down wave pattern through the middle of it until you cut through the whole potato. Pull the two wave pieces apart. Insert a slice of Havarti Dill cheese and then put the other potato slice back on top. Allow the cheese time to melt down the sides of the potato before serving.

3. Potato Skins

Soak, wash and scrub a mealy potato clean. Rub the outside with vegetable oil and bake it in the oven for 60 minutes at 400 degrees Fahrenheit. 5. As the potato lays naturally, cut it all the way in half lengthwise. Scoop out the insides with a spoon from both sides all the way down to the skin. Fill the inside of the potato skin with caramelized onion, bell pepper, tomato, eggplant and zucchini. Put the potato skin under a broiler on high for 6 minutes until the top becomes golden brown.

4. Pig Ears

Soak, wash and scrub a mealy potato clean. Rub it with Canola Oil and bake it in the oven for 60 minutes at 400 degrees Fahrenheit. 6. As the potato lays, cut the potato all the way in half lengthwise. Scoop out the contents with a spoon and then either save, discard or use the innards for another recipe. 7. Cut the two potato halves in half short ways.

Photo: Pig Ear

Deep fry the pieces in oil until crispy and golden brown. Serve with vegetarian bean chili.

5. Potato Heart

Soak, wash and scrub a waxy potato clean. Rub it with Canola Oil and bake it in the oven for 60 minutes at 400 degrees Fahrenheit. 8. Using a Chef knife cut the potato all the way in half, short ways on the bias. 9. Cut a short ways bias slice from each side.

Photo: Half Moon and Baseball Diamond

10. Cut each slice in half in the shape of a half moon. 11. Cut each half-moon in half again in the shape of a baseball diamond. 12. Stab the pieces onto the end of a skewer. Turn one of the potato halves around 180 degrees to form a heart alongside the other half then stab through the two pieces together with the skewer. Serve on a scoop of sour cream with a dash of Tabasco sauce.

6. Potato Puzzle

Soak, wash and scrub a potato clean. Rub it with Canola Oil and bake it in the oven for 60 minutes at 400 degrees Fahrenheit. 13. Using a paring knife, stab the potato halfway through in the middle. Continue to stab the potato all the way around it, rotating the blade left and right each time connecting the cut to the next one.

Photo: Forked Potato and Potato Puzzle

Pull the two potato pieces apart when you finish. Dip the end of the potato in a dried mixture of paprika, garlic salt, onion powder and pepper mixture. Deep fry the potato halves until golden brown. Serve with a demi glaze.

7. Butterflied Potato

Soak, wash and scrub a mealy potato clean. Rub it with Canola Oil and wrap it in in tin foil. Bake it in the oven for 60 minutes at 400 degrees Fahrenheit. 14. Lay the potato flat and gently smash it down with your hand. 15. Cut it only half way through lengthwise, open it like a butterfly and squeeze the two sides independently. 16. Use a fork to rake the potato innards. Serve with a dollop of sour cream, diced chives, salt and ground pepper.

8. Potato Grid

Soak, wash, and scrub a waxy potato clean. Rub it with Canola Oil and bake it in the oven for 30 minutes at 350 degrees Fahrenheit. Using a Chef knife cut the potato all the way in half lengthwise. 17. Then cut a grid of horizontal lines across the potato without piercing the skin, turn the potato 90 degrees and repeat multiple horizontal lines.

Photo: Potato Grid

Flip the potato inside out to reveal the cuts. Drizzle the grid with basil pesto and serve.

9. Potato Cones
Soak, wash and scrub a mealy potato clean. Rub it with Canola Oil and bake it in the oven for 60 minutes at 400 degrees Fahrenheit. 18. Cut the potato in half short ways in the middle. 19. Carefully scoop out the innards with a spoon, which you can either save, discard or use it for another recipe.

Photo: Potato Cone

Fill the potato skin cone with a mushroom ragout with garlic, thyme, and minced shallot.

10. Potato Basket
Soak, wash and scrub a mealy potato clean. Rub it with Canola Oil and bake it in the oven for 60 minutes at 400 degrees Fahrenheit. Cut the potato half way through the middle then half way to the middle from the other way then remove that section.

Photo: Potato Basket

20. Scoop out the inside, fill it with cut grilled corn buttered and seasoned with salt and pepper.

11. Potato Rainbow

Soak, wash and scrub a waxy potato clean. Cut the potato all the way in half through the middle then turn the potato and cut it again all the way through the other way Hollow out the pieces with a spoon.   21. Cut several horizontal lines across each piece to make arches. Keep track of the pieces as you cut them so they can be sorted out later.

Photo: Potato Rainbow

Separate the arches into three piles according to size. Parboil the pieces separately in pots of spinach, carrot, and beets to both color and flavor the pieces.   Arrange the arches smallest to largest like a rainbow when serving. Season with course sea salt.

12. Potato Feather

Soak, wash and scrub a mealy potato clean. Rub it with Canola Oil and wrap it in tin foil. Bake in the oven for 60 minutes at 350 degrees Fahrenheit. 22. Cut off one lengthwise side. 23. Cut off the other lengthwise side. 24. Turn the potato over and cut off the third side 25. And finally cut off the fourth side leaving a rectangular prism behind. 26. On the skin side cut one horizontal line through center of each piece from one end to the other. Then cut many bias cuts fanning down on both sides of the center line. Salt and pepper the pieces and serve them skewered on tooth picks so they look like feathers. To serve lightly brush them with Hoison Duck sauce.

13. Potato Stamp
Soak, wash and scrub a waxy potato clean. Rub it with Canola Oil and bake it in the oven for 60 minutes at 350 degrees Fahrenheit. 27. Cut the ends off of the potato. 28. Cut a star design into the top of the piece while removing the sides.

Photo: Potato Stamp

Dab the star end onto a drop of reduced balsamic vinegar, stamp the star design on a plate and serve together.

14. Potato Wedges and Turned Potatoes
Soak, wash and scrub a mealy potato clean. Cut the potato in half lengthwise. 29. Then cut the pieces in half again lengthwise 30. Then cut them in half again lengthwise. 31. Or cut the potato halves into thirds. 32. Finally so the wedges cook evenly, slice perpendicular lines through the flesh of the wedge so they turn up like a smile. 33. Alternate partial cuts through the skin and flesh so the wedge can stretch both ways like a snake. 34. Rotate the potato wedge 45 degrees after making each cut to have oblique cuts. 35. Cut the potato wedge in half, then cut 7 perfectly consecutive smooth lines from top to bottom using a paring knife to make a turned potato.

Photo: Turned Potatoes

Toss the pieces in parsley, thyme, rosemary, salt and pepper. Deep fry them until they are golden brown. Serve with a ketchup and horseradish sauce.

15. Steak Fries

Soak, wash and scrub a mealy potato clean. Rub it with Canola Oil and bake it in the oven for 60 minutes at 350 degrees Fahrenheit. Cut the potato in half lengthwise. 36. Cut the two halves evenly in half horizontally. 37. Or cut four wedges then make lengthwise slices and fan them out to display the cuts.

Photo: Steak Fries and Wedges

Deep fry them in oil with sweet potato fries and leeks cut the same way. Serve them covered in Old Bay Seasoning.

16. Potato Peel
Soak, wash and scrub a mealy potato clean. 38. Peel the raw potato from the top to the bottom so you have one continuous circular peel.

Photo: Potato Peel Flower

Roll the peel into a flower garnish. 39. Cut off the bottom so it stands up.

Photo: Potato Peel Strands

40. Slice the roll thinly using a Chef Knife and deep fry the seasoned strands to serve on a garden burger.

17. Boiled Potato
Soak, wash and scrub a medium starch potato clean. 41. Peel the potato making short chips all around it with a sharp peeler.

Photo: Chip Peeled Potato

Drop the whole peeled potato into salted, boiling water and cook for 25 minutes. 42. Cut the potato in half short ways to make two mounds. Serve with Espagnole Sauce.

18. 3D Potato
Soak, wash and scrub a mealy potato clean. 43. Using a Chef knife cut out a wedge of potato lengthwise. Pull the wedge towards you. Carefully cut another wedge from that piece. Pull it towards you so you can see it clearly. Continue cutting smaller and smaller wedges from each piece. Turn the potato around perhaps cutting out two or three more of these expanding potato wedges from each side. Make sure to secure each section with your hand before moving onto the next one.

Photo: 3-D Potato

Finally secure the potato with a piece of string bundled with a bunch of thyme, rosemary, and tarragon. Bake the potato for 60 minutes at 400 degrees Fahrenheit. Season with sea salt, Black Tellicherry pepper and a dollop of whipped avocado butter.

19. Assorted Baked Potato Slices

I have listed here 20 different ways to cut a scalloped potato slice but there must be at least 101 ways, the list goes on. Make sure to stretch before attempting a lot of cutting. Also try squeezing a rolled up dish towel in your hand to strengthen your wrists and hands if they get over worked. If you are using the skin of the potato, make sure to soak, wash and scrub the potato clean 44. Slice ¼" short ways potato scallops. Gently soak the potatoes in water after you cut each one remove the excess starch. 45. Peel the potato from top to bottom leaving behind lines of skin. 46. Slice the lined potato short ways. 47. Cut a spiral through a scalloped potato slice

Photo: Potato Pentagon Prism

48. Cut off five equal edges of a whole potato to form a pentagon and then slice it. 49. Cut off eight equal edges to form an octagon and slice it. 50. Use a ring mold to cut a perfectly round cylinder. 51. Use a corer to cut a perfect round through the center.

Photo: Hollow Scarred Potato Prism

52. Use a knife to scar the outside.

Photo: Scarred Cylinder Rounds

53. Slice the cylinder rounds.

Photo: Potato Curly Fries

54. Using a paring knife cut a downward spiral through the core of each round for curly fries.

Photo: Waffle Chips

55. Adjust a mandolin blade close to cut paper thin potato chips. 56. Cut waffle chips on a mandolin using a julienne blade attachment, widening the blade opening and rotating the potato 90 degrees after each cut.

Photo: Ruffled Potato Chips

57. To make a ruffled chip slice on the mandolin with a wave blade attachment. 58. Cut a ¼" scallop potato and slice it evenly on the bias many times, push the pieces over and spread them out. 59. Cut four half-moons out opposite sides of a potato and slice it to make Celtic crosses. 60. Using a corer, cut half-moons all around the edge and then slice it to make suns. 61. Use a paring knife to cut a zigzag through the middle of a scalloped potato 62. Use a cookie cutter to cut sides that mirror each other. 63. Use a paring knife to cut four triangles from opposite sides to form an X. 64. Cut off four half-moons to form a diamond. 65. Cut out five triangles to form a star. 66. Cut the skin from the outer edge of the scalloped potato slightly raising and lowering the paring knife along the way to make the wavy outline of a cloud. 67. Cut two opposing zig-zag lines through a scalloped potato that only connect at the top and the bottom to create a lightning bolt. 68. Cut two arching hooks through a scalloped potato to make a heart. 69. Using a paring knife carefully cut five overlapping flower petals to make a Plumeria Flower round.

Photo: Assorted Potato Cuts

Using a chef knife cut a potato in half lengthwise then cut several V's across the top straight edge.

Photo: Potato Crowns

70. Slice the potato to make round crowns. Oil a baking tray and evenly lay out the different cuts. Bake at 350 degrees Fahrenheit for 30 minutes until golden brown. The thicker potato slices will take longer to cook than the chips. Serve with tomato soup and melted mozzarella cheese.

20. French Fries, Shoe Strings and Picks

Soak, wash and scrub clean a mealy potato. 71. Cut off all four sides of a potato and then cut off both the top and bottom so a large block remains.   72. Cut the block into lengthwise planks ¼" thick. 73. Cut each plank lengthwise into ¼" sticks. 74. Cut each stick in half, short ways to make French Fries 2" long. 75. Cut each stick in half lengthwise for julienne cuts 1/8" x ¼". 76. Cut the julienne piece in half from one corner to the opposite corner to make pointed picks. 77. Then slice the julienne evenly lengthwise 1/16" to make shoestrings.

Photo: Matchsticks, Julienne, and Planks

Deep fry the potatoes pieces until golden brown. Serve with seasoned mayonnaise.

21. Hashbrowns
Soak, wash and scrub clean a medium starch potato. 78. Grate it on a box grater.

Photo: Grated Potato

Gather them with oil, salt and pepper. Cook them in a hot skillet until golden brown. Serve with ketchup.

22. Potato Pancakes
Soak, wash and scrub a starchy potato clean. 79. Use a grater and make short quick strokes through a whole potato.

Photo: 4 Grades of Grated Potatoes

Mix the potato pieces with milk, eggs and onions. Portion a small patty, squeeze the liquid out of it and cook it in a hot oiled skillet until its golden brown on both sides. Serve with a dollop of sour cream and apple sauce.

23. Potato Cage

Soak, wash and scrub a waxy potato clean. Cut off the ends and four sides to form a block. 80. Rotate 45 degrees and cut four sides off, on a bias, to form the point of a houses roof.

Photo: Potato Box with a Point

81. Through the box, cut a square out of the center. Push the piece through so it's hollow. 82. Turn the potato on its other side and cut another square out from the center and push out the two pieces.

Photo: Potato Cage

Stand the potato on end so it looks like a house. Stick a sprig of rosemary through a window and bake at 350 degrees Fahrenheit for 30 minutes. Handle gently, dress it in garlic oil and garnish with parsley and chives.

24. Hands and the Holy Tablet

Soak, wash and scrub a waxy potato clean. 83. Slice the potato lengthwise several times. 84. Cut one of the slices ¼" thick, then cut four partial slices lengthwise to form the fingers on a hand.

Photo: L to R. Holy Potato Slice, Small Rounds, Potato Feather, Scalloped Slice, Bias Sliced Slice, Potato Hands and a Potato Skin

85. Take another slice and punch holes through it to form a holy tablet 86. Small rounds. Place the cuts on parchment paper. Lightly drizzle with oil then roast in the oven at 350 degrees Fahrenheit for 30 minutes or until golden brown. Serve with Lime Basil Aioli.

25. Potato Balls
Soak, wash and scrub a medium starch potato clean. Cut it all the way in half lengthwise. 87. Use a melon baller and scoop out the insides making many small round potato balls.

Photo: Potato Balls

Cook them in an oiled skillet until they are golden brown and crisp. Serve them with dollop of whipped garlic herb butter.

26. Chain Link
Soak, wash and scrub a waxy potato clean. Cut a potato into a block removing four sides plus the top and bottom. Visualize two planks inner connected. One is horizontal and the other is vertical. Cut away all excess potato besides the two inner

connected planks. Now visualize two chain links push together within the planks. Carefully cut away the potato connecting the two links. 88. Carefully cut through the middle to release the two pieces. Round the off edges to resemble a chain link.

Photo: Potato Chain Link

Soak the potato chain link in a simmering vegetable stock. Cook for 5 minutes. Handle gently.

27. Potato Head

Soak, wash and scrub a mealy potato clean. The only potato in this book that will not be edible. 89. Cut a hole in the top of a potato, big enough to fit a candle inside. Save the piece for later. Cut a small piece off the bottom of a potato so it stands up. Using a corer and a spoon cut out the insides of the potato. Make sure not to cut through to the bottom, make it flat. Cut a face into the front of the potato to see into the insides.

Photo: Potato Head

Light a candle and carefully put it inside. Put the top back on and admire at night.

28. Medium Dice Whipped Potatoes

Soak, wash and scrub a mealy potato clean. Cut off the four sides, top and bottom of the potato. 90. Cut the potato in half short ways. 91. Cut the two blocks in half again into tiles ¾". 92. Cut the tiles in half to make bricks. 93. Cut the bricks in half to make ½" medium dice potatoes. Cook the potato in salted boiling water. Cook until tender and then drain the hot water.

Photo: Whipped Potato

94. Put the potatoes pieces in a bowl and whip them until they are fluffy using a mixer. Incorporate cooked taro to add color and flavor to the potatoes.

29. Potato Juice

Soak, wash and scrub a waxy potato clean. Peel the potato. Using a Chef knife cut the potato into thick slices. 95. Roughly chop the potato into small pieces.

Photo: Potato Juice

96. Put the potato through a juicer with kale, carrots, beets and radish. Serve with honey.

30. Whole Holy Potato

Soak, wash and scrub clean a medium starch potato. 97. Use a corer and cut holes all the way through a whole potato.

Photo: Holy Potato

Cut holes also through yam, sweet potato and carrots. Replace the holes with other vegetable cores. Wrap the potato in tin foil and bake in an oven for 30 minutes at 350 degrees Fahrenheit. Serve covered in beef gravy.

31. Minced Potato

Soak, wash and scrub clean a mealy potato. 98. Use a grater and cut a potato in its smaller side. 99. Then dice it further all the way until it is minced. Mix the potato with minced onion, garlic and parsnip. Cook in a hot oiled frying pan. Garnish with a sprig of fresh tarragon.

Photo: Minced Potato

32. Potato Puree

Soak, wash and scrub clean a mealy potato. Using a Chef knife cut a potato into long skinny pieces lengthwise 1/16". 100. Dice the potato pieces further into small dice. Quickly boil the potatoes in salted boiling water.

Photo: Potato Puree

101. Strain the water and use a food processor to puree the potato with cooked onions, garlic, cream and butter to make potato soup.

EPILOG

Writing this potato book has been quite a long journey. I began this project in 2009 on a whim. I hand wrote a book containing every possible thing I could think of doing with a potato. I was torn between writing another potato cook book or a book about knife skills and creative cooking. Eventually it morphed into what it is today, focusing mostly on the many ways to prepare a potato for cooking. I have come to appreciate potatoes more than ever for their contribution to the culinary world. They have fed the world many times over throughout our history on this planet. We all should be grateful and continue to incorporate the potato into our diet as our ancestors have done. I hope this book has in some way inspired you. Cheers.

POTATO CUT INDEX

The following list of cuts correspond with each example of food. It is by no means the only way to cut these foods but it gives you at least one idea.

The Cuts   **Examples**

1. Poked — Sweet Potato
2. In Half Lengthwise On Edge — Brussel Sprouts
3. Potato Skin — Papaya
4. Mashed — Cranberries
5. Waves — Cake
6. In Half Lengthwise As It Lays — Pineapple
7. Pig Ears — Bell Pepper
8. Whole Bias — Egg Roll
9. Scallop Bias — Green Onion
10. Half Moon — Daikon
11. Baseball Diamond — Hearts of Palm
12. Skewered — Beef
13. Stabbed — Beets
14. Smashed — Banana
15. Butterfly — Scrimp
16. Raked — Coconut
17. Grid — Mango
18. Cut in Half Short ways — Passion Fruit
19. Cones — Tomato
20. Basket — Peach
21. Rainbow — Cabbage
22. Topless Block — Fig
23. Two Sided Block — Steak
24. Three Sided Block — Pomegranate
25. Four Sided Block — Corn
26. Feather — Eggplant
27. Endless Block — Kiwi
28. Stamp — Radish
29. Wedges 4x — Bread Fruit
30. Wedges 8x — Lemon
31. Wedges 6x — Lime

32. Accordion	Hot Dog
33. Snake	Bean Pods
34. Oblique	Rhubarb
35. Turned Potato	Broccoli Stem
36. Steak Fries	Kohlrabi
37. Wedge Fan	Avocado
38. Spiral Peel	Mandarin
39. Flower Roll	Pear
40. Single Peel Sliced	Basil
41. Short Peel	Parsnip
42. Cone Mound	Melon
43. 3D Wedge	Guava
44. Scallop	Fennel
45. Lined Peel	Squash
46. Lined Peel Slice	Cucumber
47. Scalloped Spiral	Horseradish
48. Pentagon Slice	Carrot
49. Octagon Slice	Quince
50. Cylinder	Orange
51. Hollowed Cylinder	Apple
52. Cylinder Scarred	Pineapple
53. Hollowed Cylinder Sliced	Leeks
54. Curly Fries	Rutabaga
55. Chips	Turnip
56. Waffle Chips	Yacon
57. Ruffled Chips	Watercress
58. Scalloped Bias Slice	Turmeric
59. Celtic Cross	Nectarine
60. Sun	Dragon Fruit
61. Zig-Zag Slice	Grapes
62. Mirrored Slice	Mushroom
63. X	Chocolate
64. Diamond	Ti Leaf
65. Star	Grapefruit
66. Cloud	Jicama
67. Lightning	Crackers
68. Heart	Beet
69. Flower Round	Strawberry
70. Crown Slice	Dates

71. Cubed Block	Yellowfin Tuna
72. Plank	Sandwich Roll
73. Batonnet	Celery
74. French Fries	Chicory
75. Julienne	Lettuce
76. Picks	Sugarcane
77. Shoestring- Allumettes	Leeks
78. Grated	Chili Pepper
79. Chipped	Parmesan
80. Box and Steeple	Sweet Potato
81. Cubed Block Hollowed	Dahlia
82. Cage	Yam
83. Slice Lengthwise	Okra
84. Hand	Endive
85. Hole Punch	Olive
86. Small Rounds	Peas
87. Potato Balls	Cantaloupe
88. Chain Link	Sassafras Root
89. Potato Head	Pumpkin
90. Large Boxes	Crotons
91. Tiles	Onions
92. Brick	Butternut Squash
93. Medium Dice	Jerusalem Artichoke
94. Whipped	Taro
95. Rough Chop	Spinach
96. Juiced	Kale
97. Holy Whole	Cheddar Cheese
98. Fine Grated	Ginger
99. Minced	Garlic
100. Small Dice- Brunoises	Jalapeno
101. Puree	Black Beans

BIBLIOGRAPHY

Bruce Weinstein, and Mark Scarbrough. *The Ultimate Potato Book.* New York, NY: Harper Collins, 2009

Hielke De Jong, *The Complete Book of Potatoes.* New York, NY: Workman Pub Company, 2011

Alan Romans, *The Potato Book.* London, England: Frances Lincoln Limited, 2005

COPYRIGHT 2015 BENJAMIN JAMES FREEMAN-PRICHARD

Made in the USA
San Bernardino, CA
15 November 2015